UNDERS

G000167822

UNDERSTANDING
GUIDANCE

by

Selwyn Hughes

**CWR, 10 Brooklands Close,
Sunbury-on-Thames,
Middx TW16 7DX**

NATIONAL DISTRIBUTORS
Australia: Christian Marketing Pty Ltd., PO Box 154,
North Geelong, Victoria 3215.
Tel: (052) 786100
Canada: Christian Marketing Canada Ltd.,
PO Box 550, Virgil, Ontario LOS ITO.
Tel: 416 641 0631
Republic of Ireland: Merrion Press Ltd.,
10 D'Olier Street, Dublin.
Tel & Fax: 773316
Malaysia: Salvation Book Centre, (M) Sdn. Bhd.,
23 Jalan SS2/64, 47300 Petaling Jaya, Selangor
New Zealand: CWR (NZ), PO Box 4108,
Mount Maunganui 3030.
Tel: (075) 757412
Singapore: Alby Commercial Enterprises Pte Ltd.,
Garden Hotel, 14 Balmoral Road, Singapore 1025
Southern Africa: CWR (Southern Africa), PO Box 43,
Kenilworth 7745, South Africa.
Tel: (021) 7612560

Typeset by J&L Composition Ltd, Filey, North Yorkshire

Printed in Great Britain by Richard Clay Ltd,
Bungay, Suffolk

ISBN 1-85345-037-5

Contents

INTRODUCTION

"I will instruct you and teach you the way you should go; I will counsel you with my eye upon you." (Psalm 32:8, RSV)

Does God really guide and direct the lives of His children? Is it possible to believe that the great Creator and Sustainer of the universe takes a personal interest in the affairs of each one of His people on this microscopic earth? And if so, how does He go about the task of showing us His plans and purposes for our lives? These are the questions which so many people are asking and with which we shall come to grips in this book.

Many Christians know little or nothing about personal guidance from God. They go from event to event and live a kind of hand-to-mouth spiritual existence – a spiritual and moral opportunism. They have little or no sense of destiny, of mission. Hence their impact upon life is feeble. Only people who have a sense of mission and who know what it means to be guided by God accomplish things. If we do not have a sense of being led, we become victims of our circumstances; we are circumstance-directed instead of Christ-directed.

When the Israelites fashioned and worshipped the

golden calf and Moses pleaded for them, God told them that He would not go before them, but that He would send His angel to be their guide:

"I will send an angel before you and drive out the Canaanites, Amorites, Hittites, Perizzites, Hivites and Jebusites. Go up to the land flowing with milk and honey. But I will not go with you, because you are a stiff-necked people and I might destroy you on the way." (Exodus 33:2–3, NIV).

For a time their religion became a second-hand affair, through angels instead of direct contact with God. How tragic! Guidance, as one preacher put it, "is not a spiritual luxury for rare souls but the minimum necessity for every Christian." "Those who are led by the Spirit of God are sons of God" (Romans 8:14, NIV). No leadership – no sonship. Dare to believe it – the Almighty God, at whose word the great planets spin and whirl, condescends to say to you: "I will counsel you with my eye upon you" (Psalm 32:8).

Let us establish one thing at the start of this book. We may well have allowed ourselves to slip away from God's direct guidance on our lives. Pray this prayer with me as we explore afresh and come to understand anew the guidance and the will of God.

PRAYER:
O God, forgive me if I have allowed my faith to become second-hand and vague, instead of first-hand and vital. I want so much to know the sense of being led, the sense that I am in direct contact with You. Help me to know it. For Jesus' sake. Amen.

CHAPTER 1

ANYBODY GOING ANYWHERE?

"The Lord will guide you always . . . You will be like a well-watered garden, like a spring whose waters never fail." (Isaiah 58:11, NIV)

If life is to be at its best we must have, as one writer put it, "a sense of instrumentation" – a feeling that we are carrying out purposes beyond our own, of fulfilling a will that is infinite and ultimate. One of the greatest urgencies in the Christian life today is to regain the sense of being led. Without that, life lacks a goal and the dynamic to move towards that goal.

The men in a certain church organised a supper for themselves and, being unused to catering, gave contradictory orders to the caretaker. Naturally, he became upset and voiced his feelings to the organisers. One of the men remarked facetiously, "If you get upset with us, what do you do when the women are here?" He replied, "That's simple; I just put my mind in neutral and go where I'm pushed."

A great many Christians live their lives like that; they throw their minds into neutral and go where circumstances push them. They have no sense of being led. Or else they allow other people's actions to determine their conduct and behaviour.

Jesus warned us about allowing other people to determine our conduct when He said, "If someone strikes you on the right cheek, turn to him the other also" (Matthew 5:39, NIV). In other words, don't use his weapons, but keep your own.

And what are the Christian's weapons? They are many, not the least being the choice to be directed by God and not by circumstances, to be impelled from within rather than compelled from without. We Christians must work from principles, not pressures. Every Christian should live a God-guided life – for if God *is*, then He should be in everything that concerns us – directing, controlling, inspiring.

If we are not God-led, we shall probably be mob-led. We will react, rather than act. If we are not led by God, then we become led by circumstances, things or people. It is imperative that we Christians regain the sense of being led, for without it life turns dull and insipid.

Some time ago there came into my hands the report of a conference in the United States where the leading members of a certain denomination were gathered together and asked to share openly and honestly their views on the subject of divine guidance. The conference began with the expected defensiveness, but after a few days the Holy Spirit broke through into the midst of that group with the result that many of them stood up and confessed that they lacked the sense of being led. A minister who was there wrote: "Some of us were well-known for our executive ability and efficiency, we were people who were admired by our congregations, but under the scrutiny of the Spirit we were shown to be agitated, half-committed, wistful, self-placating seekers who were more taken up with having our own way than finding God's way. Indeed, many of us came to see that our

11

religion was a second-hand affair, and that our Christian lives were *dull and insipid* (italics mine). We were being guided more by our inner needs than by the constraints of God."

Before we become too judgmental, let's pause for a moment and ask ourselves the question: Is my life dull and insipid? Do I lack a sense of being led? I say again, if you are not guided by God you will be guided by something else – by others or perhaps yourself.

The stars that destroy

The growth of astrology in our Western society is a sign of the lack of firsthand contact with God. Now that God has faded in the minds of most of the men and women in our nations, and Christian principles do not have such a strong hold on our society, people are finding their direction in the stars.

Turning to the stars for guidance is always a sign of decay – mentally and spiritually. God is very clear concerning His mind on astrology. It is sheer materialism to believe that life is determined by lumps of matter floating about in space. Astrology – not astronomy – laid its hand on the mind of Greece and paralysed it. The Greek mind was sharp and brilliant, bravely facing the facts of life, until it turned to the stars for comfort and support. A well-known missionary to India writes: "The mind of India was a creative mind, producing the most amazing Sanskrit literature, until astrology made it sterile and non-creative by turning it toward the stars instead of toward the facts of life."

Disturbing as it is to see increasing numbers in our modern-day society daily consulting horoscopes, what is more disturbing is the knowledge that some Christians adopt this practice too. Some regard it as an innocent and harmless pastime. Not so. Astrology will drain and damage your spiritual life and lead you not toward God, but away from Him. Why settle for being guided by the stars when you can be guided by the God who created them?

When God's people lose the sense of being guided, they turn to anything for guidance. Of all the things men and women turn to for guidance, astrology is one of the most devastating, for it means that moral considerations have been abandoned and one's destiny is decided by the position of the stars.

I have no hesitation in saying that any nation – or individual – which adopts the methods of astrology to obtain guidance will soon find itself in moral disillusionment and intellectual decay. We are told that several million people in Britain daily consult a horoscope. The newspapers that publish these daily charts are contributing to this moral and intellectual decay. There is little difference between an ancient pagan bowing before a stone idol, asking for its blessing, and a modern pagan studying charts that depict the movements of lumps of matter in the sky which he thinks guide his life.

My concern here, however, is not so much with secular society, but with those Christians who may be tempted to turn to horoscopes for their daily guidance. The stars which God has made can separate us from Him if we make the stars our guide rather than letting God reveal Himself to us through

Christ and His Word. Quite simply, gazing at the stars in order to find guidance constitutes the sin of idolatry, and *must* be repented of. The only horoscope we should be interested in is our destiny in Christ. I consider the influence of horoscopes on lives to be one of the most dangerous things there can be from allowing God to have His way in lives. Have you read horoscopes? If so, pray this prayer now, to be free of their influence and to be open to God.

PRAYER

O God, I see how easy it is, when I have lost sight of You, to turn to other things for guidance and I renounce right now every other form of guidance in my life, and put my trust directly in You. It's done, Father. I am yours to guide. Amen.

Freedom from worry

Lack of clear guidance so often leads to worry. I am often asked in letters and in interviews: what is the secret of emancipation from worry? How may one shed a fretful and fearful attitude to life? The answer I usually give is this, *live the guided life*. As soon as one understands the importance of allowing one's life to be guided by God and seeks His direction and control, it is not long before one experiences a deep inner peace. "... He who has compassion on them will guide them and lead them beside springs of water" (Isaiah 49:10, NIV).

As Dr W.E. Sangster put it: "Not to feel the whole burden of responsible decision; not to find one's

mind a constant battleground of contending forces;
not to be haunted by the fear of the consequences as
one anticipates a grave mistake – that is half the
journey to the land of inner peace." When we are
sensitive to the commands and counsel of God, and
feel our own powers of reason and insight clarified by
the light of His presence, we arrive at what one writer
describes as "the Canaan of His perfect love". Here
there is still need for toil, but it is toil amid tranquillity;
it is the "rest that remains for the people of God"
(Hebrews 4:9).

Contrast this with the stress and strain of those
who feel no co-operative help from above; tossing on
seas of uncertainty, and coming to their decisions
with frantic and unquiet minds. Sometimes their very
indecision settles the matter. "This is the only thing I
can do now," they say. Indecision then becomes
decision. They drift on with a spurious sense of relief,
and try to convince themselves that this is the way
life should be lived. How different for those who say,
"We are not our own; we were bought at a price".
They are the people of peace.

> "Do you not know that your body is a temple of the
> Holy Spirit, who is in you, whom you have re-
> ceived from God? You are not your own; you were
> bought at a price. Therefore honour God with your
> body" (1 Corinthians 6:19–20, NIV).

The message I have been trying to get across, in
one way and another, during this first chapter, is this:
we Christians must regain the sense of being led. And
why? Because without that sense of being led, life is

aimless – it lacks a goal and the dynamic to move on to that goal.

A man stood up at the end of a small Christian conference and said, "Anybody got a car going anywhere?" Everyone laughed, for they knew that a car doesn't just go anywhere – it must go somewhere. Many Christians are just concerned with going rather than going somewhere. As long as they are moving, they are not particularly concerned about the direction or the goal. To be successful in our Christian lives, we must not only move, but move in the right direction and in accordance with divine guidance.

Some time ago, I reread *The Jade Gate*, the story of Mildred Cable and Evangeline and Francesca French who, early this century, travelled to China bearing the good news of the Gospel. It is a wonderful story of hardship and fortitude. Strong men wept when, in 1926, these three women returned home and told their story to the Christians in Britain. Why did they go? Because of guidance: "a secret consciousness of being in receipt of Sealed Orders – to proceed to the great North West to a place at present unknown". Let no one feel, however, that only the great are guided. Our habit of reaching for a classic illustration may sometimes give that impression. God guides more of His servants in the paths of obscurity than He guides in the floodlit way. "To shine on those living in darkness . . . to guide our feet into the way of peace" (Luke 1:79, NIV).

CHAPTER 2

NO
SHORT
CUTS

"I guide you in the way of wisdom and lead you along straight paths." (Proverbs 4:11, NIV)

Guidance is the very essence of Christianity. As we have said, it is not a spiritual luxury for a few, it is for every Christian.

We must turn to face an extremely interesting and vital question: if divine guidance is so important and so necessary to effective Christian living, why is it so difficult to obtain? Of course, there will be some who will respond to that question by saying, "Guidance presents no difficulties to me: I ask God to guide me – and He does. It is as simple as that." Others, however – perhaps most of us – would view the whole subject of divine guidance as "a riddle, wrapped up in a mystery, inside an enigma".

Gimmicks, formulas and techniques

One reason why some Christians find it difficult to discover divine guidance is because they mistakenly view it as something that can only be obtained by the use of formulas and techniques. Some of the ways Christians adopt to discover God's guidance for their lives are so ridiculous that if they were not employed with such sincerity and devotion, they would be downright hilarious. I heard about a lady, seeking guidance as to whether or not she should go on a

Holy Land tour, who read in the travel brochure that the flight from London to Tel Aviv would be on a Boeing 747. The next morning she awoke and looked at her clock. It was 7:47 am precisely. This she took as her "sign" from God that He wanted her to go to the Holy Land. You may smile at this, but I wonder what methods you adopt in your attempt to discover God's will? God guides – but never by gimmicks.

Christians fail to get guidance because they mistakenly view it as a matter of formulas or techniques.

A deacon in a small church in the United States was asked by the congregation to take over the leadership of the church after the minister left. He agreed to do so but, although a good preacher, he felt somewhat inadequate for the task because he did not have a divinity degree. He toyed with the idea of buying a theological degree from what in America is called "a degree mill" – an institution which specialises in selling unaccredited degrees. He prayed about the matter and one day, when reading 1 Timothy 3:13 in the Authorised Version, his mind was made up. This is what he read: "For they that have used the office of a deacon well purchase to themselves a good degree."

Unbelievable? Well, how about this? I heard recently of a young woman who felt that the Lord had called her to be a missionary, but wasn't sure about the country or the people to whom she should go. She got the "guidance" she needed when, driving in London one day, her car ran out of petrol outside the Philippine Embassy. This, she decided, was the Lord's way of showing her that she should become a missionary to the Philippines.

Lest I over-simplify the problem, let me make it

clear that there are many areas of legitimate concern that are not specifically addressed in the Bible, and deeply committed Christians are often at a loss to know what to do. However, just as there are no "short cuts" on a straight road, so there are no magic formulas for knowing the will of God, but there are patterns as Paul notes in writing to Timothy: "What you heard from me, keep as the pattern of sound teaching, with faith and love in Christ Jesus" (2 Timothy 1:13, NIV).

Our wants

Another reason why guidance fails to come is because, although we may ask God to guide us, what we really want deep down in our hearts is God's stamp of approval on our own selfish desires. I once heard of a man who prayed this prayer: "Lord, choose me a wife, but let it be Mary." I am not saying, of course, that every decision we make in life has to be submitted to God for His approval for, if that were the case, we probably would never get dressed in the mornings.

Many of the desires that spring into our minds are tainted with self-centredness and self-interest, and it is perilously easy to bring them to God, not for His examination, but for His unqualified approval. We are like the little boy who prayed that God would make Birmingham the capital of England. When his mother asked why he prayed that prayer, he replied that he had put down that city as the capital on his examination paper!

We must fix it in our minds that if we are wanting

God's guidance for our lives, then we must be willing to be guided, not to our ends, but to God's ends. Jesus was our model, our example for this: "For I have come down from heaven not to do my will but to do the will of him who sent me" (John 6:38, NIV).

A woman was told by her pastor during a counselling session, "Now say to God: 'Let anything happen to me that You want to happen to me.'" She looked at the counsellor aghast: "Oh no," she said, "I don't want that." She thought, as indeed do many Christians, that God's will for her would lie along the line of the disagreeable. The fact is that God couldn't will anything for us except our highest good – and still be God. God's will is in our highest interest at all times, in all places and under all circumstances.

Crisis versus continuous

There are many Christians who fail to see that guidance is not something that happens only in a crisis, but something that happens in the continuous. We must be willing to be guided by God, not merely now and then, but as a life proposition. It is difficult to get light in a crisis if you are not willing to get light in the continuous.

Some Christians view God as someone upon whom they call when in a crisis – to get them out of scrapes in which they have become entangled by their own self-will. A Swedish literary woman wanted God to show her the next step in her career and at length, in a surge of abandon that broke through all her reserve, she shouted out to God: "Why don't You speak to me?" The words she got in reply were these: "How could you expect me to speak when you have gagged me for so long?"

Don't gag God in the continuous and expect Him to speak to you in the crisis. The plan of your life might be unfolded in a moment of sudden insight, or it might be a gradual unfolding. Yet the gradual unfolding may be the highest form of guidance.

Someone said that the text, "The steps of a good man are ordered by the Lord" (Psa. 37:23, AV) means "every two and a half feet". The psalmist said, "Your word is a lamp to my feet" (Psa. 119:105, NIV). Note, "a lamp to my feet", not a spotlight, but just enough light by which to see the next step. The advice given to me by one of my tutors in College has never left me: in order to get guidance in a crisis, remain in the will of God in the continuous: "I being in the way, the Lord led me" (Genesis 24:27, AV).

Methods versus relationships

Another way in which we make it difficult for ourselves to receive divine guidance is our tendency to see it in terms of methods rather than in terms of a relationship. This is an extremely important point. Perhaps this is why the Bible contains very little specific advice about guidance, but a great deal on the proper way to maintain a loving relationship with our Creator.

If there is one thing I learned in marriage, it was that the highest form of communication between my wife and myself was a picture of the intimacy God desires to have with me. In the early days of marriage, I made many momentous decisions without consulting my wife, unaware of the fact that shutting her out of the decision-making process caused her immeasurable sadness and pain. I discovered later that she didn't want to make up my mind for me, but she did long for a conscious and willing acceptance of her presence and a recognition of her own decision-making ability. As I became aware of this, and as we had to make decisions concerning the home or the family, we thought them through together. When the decision was finally reached, both of us were sometimes quite unsure who contributed what to the ultimate result. Indeed, to even raise the point – who contributed what – would seem strangely irrelevant to intimacy. We knew full well that, during the decision-making process, we maintained our independence, and yet somehow we arrived at a joint decision. In the intimacy of marriage, we catch a glimpse of the intimacy longed for by God. God is the Lover, we are the Beloved; therefore the way we communicate is as important as the content of it.

Personal decision-making

A further reason why Christians struggle over the question of divine guidance is because they fail to see that, on occasions, God wants us to develop our own decision-making processes. I am not speaking now of those rare occasions when human wisdom is insufficient for the task, but of the ordinary perplexities of life when, with a little thought and contemplation, we could think matters through without the active help of God. I sometimes find, when counselling, that indecisive people yearn for me to make up their minds for them. At such times I have to draw back from playing the parent role, because such people long for someone to make important decisions for them. Such counsellees need, not so much advice, but encouragement to use their own decision-making processes.

This kind of situation, in which I have found myself many times, has highlighted for me the reasons why sometimes God does not tell us forthrightly which decision is the right one. (I am speaking here of morally neutral issues, of course. Anything revealed in Scripture needs no further guidance.) God refrains from doing so because He is committed to guiding us in such a way that will develop spontaneity in us. The development of character, rather than direction in this, that and the other, is always the primary purpose of our loving heavenly Father. Be assured of this, if God hesitates to intervene in your life, it is only because He sees that to do so in that particular instance will jeopardise your freedom.

Divine abdication

C.S. Lewis hinted at God's hesitance to intervene in some situations when he said: "He seems to do nothing of Himself which He can possibly delegate to His creatures. He commands us to do slowly and blunderingly what He could do perfectly and in the twinkling of an eye. . . Perhaps we do not fully realise the problem, so to call it, of enabling finite free wills to coexist with Omnipotence. It seems to involve at every moment a sort of 'divine abdication'."

Perhaps here we have the final key as to why the

issue of guidance causes so much frustration and bewilderment among Christians. Is it not a secret desire of us all, when faced with issues that are not covered by the directions of Scripture, to be told in our prayer time exactly what we should do? There are, of course, those blessed occasions when God quite clearly speaks to us and makes known His guidance, but we have to admit that there are other times when He does not. Can it be that on those occasions, when no clear direction comes, it is because at that particular moment, in those particular circumstances, our heavenly Father is saying to us: "In the interests of your own personal development, this is something I want you to think through yourself"?

Guidance, then, is guidance into our highest development and achievement. And if at times He sees that our ability to make decisions is being impaired by His guidance, He does not hesitate to stand back.

CHAPTER 3

GOD'S 'INDIVIDUAL' WILL

". . . 'The God of our fathers has chosen you to know his will. . .'" (Acts 22:14, NIV)

We cannot understand guidance fully unless we come to grips with a question which has been widely discussed in Christian circles: does God have an "individual" will for each of our lives? The issue has been under discussion since a book was published a few years ago, entitled *Decision Making and the Will of God* (Multnomah Press: USA). The author, Garry Friesen, claims that the traditional view, that God has an "individual" will for our lives, is Biblically untenable. We need to discuss this issue in some depth.

An alternative view

Garry Friesen is a committed evangelical who believes wholeheartedly in the authority of Scripture, but by making this statement he stirred up a storm in the Christian community. He described his book as "a Biblical alternative to the traditional view". This raised the question: what exactly is the traditional view of divine guidance?

Briefly, it runs like this. God's will can be divided into three categories: (1) His sovereign will, (2) His moral will, and (3) His individual will. God's *sovereign* will is the predetermined plan which He has for the ages, and is always fulfilled. It will not be frustrated by men, angels, or anything else: "All the peoples of the earth are regarded as nothing. He does as he pleases with the powers of heaven and the peoples of the earth. No-one can hold back his hand or say to him: 'What have you done?'" (Daniel 4:35, NIV). God's *moral* will is the plan revealed in the Scriptures, the moral commands which teach us how we ought to live and what we ought to believe. God's *individual* will is the ideal, detailed life-plan which God has uniquely designed for every believer. This plan encompasses the decisions we make and is the basis of God's daily guidance. These, then, are the three aspects of God's will as accepted by the majority of evangelical Christians, and the view which has been held by most believers throughout the centuries.

We can only know as much of God's sovereign will as He permits us to see, as, for example, in Biblical prophecy; and usually we recognise it only after it has happened. If you want to know God's sovereign will for the past, then just pick up a history book, and there it is. If something happened in history, it was part of His plan. Many of the older theologians referred to God's sovereign will as His "secret will", contrasting it with His revealed will which we find in the Bible.

With regard to the moral will of God, however, it is possible to know not just a part of it, but the whole. The Bible reveals *one hundred per cent* of God's moral will. You don't need to ask for guidance on the *moral* will of God, because God has given it in Scripture. If you are thinking about cheating on your taxes so that you can give more money to the work of God, you don't need to ask for the Lord's direction as He has already given it. God will never lead you to do something that is against His moral will as revealed in the Bible.

Although the Bible gives *general* instructions which affect all of life, there is need for guidance in *personal* matters. For instance, the Bible forbids a Christian to marry a non-Christian, but it does not indicate which particular person one should marry, or for that matter, whether a specific believer ought to marry at all. These personal decisions are *influenced* by God's moral will, but have to be determined by finding God's individual will.

Garry Friesen argues that the will of God must be seen, not in three perspectives, but two – His *sovereign* will and His *moral* will. There is no Biblical support, he says, for the idea of God's 'individual' will, and the concept of a personal plan for every Christian's life is not to be found in Scripture. He goes further and says that if he is right, then many believers are investing a great deal of time and energy searching for something that is non-existent. "It simply will not do," he claims, "to *assume* that God has a unique plan for each life that must be discovered as the basis for decision-making."

He concludes that God's moral will, as fully revealed in the Bible, is all that is necessary for a Christian to do the will of God on this earth, and where no specific command or principle is given, the believer is free and responsible to choose his or her own course of action. Whenever the Bible encourages Christians to know the will of God, says Friesen, it is referring to His moral will as already revealed in the Scriptures.

Four propositions

Garry Friesen has certainly shaken up the thinking in evangelical circles on the subject of decision-making (not a bad thing, you might say) and it will do us no harm to reconsider our position in relation to this compelling thought that states God does not have an "individual" will for our lives, and, in searching for it, we are looking for something that doesn't exist. In order that you might comprehend this alternative view of divine guidance – for, believe me, you are going to come across it sooner or later – let me state it in the way it is set out in Friesen's book. It demands some close thinking, so follow me carefully.

He claims the teaching of Scripture, as relating to guidance, can be summed up in these four propositions. (1) In those areas specifically addressed by the Bible, the revealed commands of God – His moral will – are to be obeyed. (2) In those areas where the Bible gives no command or principle – morally neutral decisions – the believer is free to choose his own course of action. Any decision made within the moral will of God is acceptable to God. (3) In non-moral decisions, the objective of the Christian is to make wise decisions on the basis of spiritual expediency. (4) In all decisions the believer should humbly submit, in advance, to the outworkings of God's sovereign will as it touches each decision.

The reason why so many Christians are confused when it comes to personal decisions, says Friesen, is not because they are unable to find the "individual" will of God, but because they fail to gain a good understanding of the principles of God's Word.

Knowing those principles, he claims, allows God to work within a believer, enabling him to make good and wise decisions.

Which view is right?

Now that we have pulled the two main views concerning divine guidance into focus, it is time to ask ourselves: which is right? The fact is that both of them contain a degree of truth, but the truths need to be drawn together to form a more complete whole. Although I do not agree with some of Friesen's conclusions, I am appreciative of his contribution, because he has made me, and many others, rethink our position in relation to this important matter.

Hegel, the philosopher, said that to arrive at truth we have to look first at the thesis, the proposition to be maintained; then the antithesis, the countering argument; and then the synthesis, the blending together of both arguments. This is the method I propose to adopt now in answering some of the issues raised by the question we posed at the beginning of this chapter: does God have an "individual" will for each of our lives?

The strength of the traditional view is its insistence that God does have an "individual" will for each of His children: its weakness, however, is its claim that God wants to be involved in every one of His children's decisions no matter how trivial or unimportant. God is *interested* in the tiniest details of our lives, but He does not want us to look to Him for guidance on every decision we are called upon to make. If God's "individual" will covered every single detail of our lives – the shoe we should put on first in the morning, and the road we should travel to our place of employment – our personalities would soon become stunted and cramped. God wants to guide us, but not to override us.

What, then, is the strength and the weakness of the alternative view, as put forward by Garry Friesen? Its strength lies in its emphasis on the need to absorb the principles of Scripture, so that we learn to make wise spiritual decisions in matters that are outside the scope of the Bible. Its weakness is its failure to recognise that God directs His children, not only through the Bible, but also through the witness of His Spirit speaking directly to their hearts.

God's will is general and personal

We now return to our original question and ask again: does God have an "individual" will for each of His children? Despite the insistence of the alternative view that God does not have a personal will for His people, it is quite clear, to me at least, that the Bible claims He does. Many witnesses speak to confirm this. For centuries, men and women have ventured on this concept, sought the promised guidance and testified that God was as good as His word. The Bible is full of such stories. Peep into the Old Testament: think of Abraham's servant finding Rebekah, of the stories of Moses, Samuel and the prophets, all witnessing to the fact that God's guidance is particular as well as general, and willingly given to the limit of man's capacity to receive and understand.

The same can be seen in the New Testament also.

Think of Philip and the Ethiopian eunuch, or of Ananias and Saul, or of Peter and Cornelius, all these stories are substantially false if God does not guide His people by personal contact. And what of the example of Jesus? He got His guidance, not only from Scripture, but from direct contact with God in prayer. How did He know how to be in the right place at the right time? He was *guided*. He taught His disciples to pray, "Your will be done" (Matthew 6:5–15), a prayer which presupposes the possibility of *knowing* that will; and knowing it, one must assume, not as a mass of vague sentiment, but with some concreteness and precision.

All through the ages, men and women have believed that God has condescended to guide them. In each generation, godly people have claimed that the disciplines of Bible reading and prayer have led them to know God's guidance in their lives. Augustine and Luther, St Teresa and Wesley, these and countless others vouch for its truth. If these facts are not conclusive, then consider this: is it conceivable that the God who plans every blade of grass to be different and every snowflake unique would not take the same, if not more, loving care in the development of His blood-bought children? We are of far more value to God than other created things. "Look at the birds of the air; they do not sow or reap or store away in barns, and yet your heavenly Father feeds them. Are you not much more valuable than they?" (Matthew 6:26, NIV). Be assured of this, your Father *has* a unique and personal plan for your life.

CHAPTER 4

HEARING, HOLDING AND PRACTISING

"All Scripture is God-breathed and is useful for teaching, rebuking, correcting and training in righteousness" (2 Timothy 3:16, NIV).

It is time now to come to grips with the question: *how* does God guide us? A letter I received from a schoolteacher said: "I am at an impasse in my life. I just don't know which way to go. How – *how* do I find God's will for my life?"

Guided by God's Word

How, then, does God go about the task of steering us toward His perfect will and purpose for our lives? He does it primarily through His Word, the Bible. *Scripture provides the single most important guide and checkpoint for our lives.* I love the way the "Living Bible" translates 2 Timothy 3:16, "The whole Bible was given to us by inspiration from God and is useful to teach us what is true and to make us realise what is wrong in our lives; it straightens us out and helps us do what is right."

There are many verses in Scripture which emphasise that God's Word is the major checkpoint for our lives. Paul tells us in Galatians 1:6–9 that even if an angel were to supernaturally appear whose message contradicted the already revealed will of God in the Scriptures, one should hold to the Bible rather than the angel's message: "I am astonished that you are so quickly deserting the one who called you by the grace of Christ and are turning to a different gospel – which is really no gospel at all. Evidently some people are throwing you into confusion and are trying to pervert the gospel of Christ. But even if we or an angel from heaven should preach a gospel other than the one we preached to you, let him be eternally condemned! As we have already said, so now I say again: If anybody is preaching to you a gospel other than what you accepted, let him be eternally condemned!" (NIV).

The Jews of Berea were commended for listening to Paul's preaching with open and attentive hearts, and then checking the Scriptures to see if what was spoken was correct: "Now the Bereans were of more noble character than the Thessalonians, for they received the message with great eagerness and examined the Scriptures every day to see if what Paul said was true" (Acts 17:11, NIV).

In the Scriptures God has given us 66 books filled with principles and precepts which provide a much more objective set of guidelines than those that come from impulses or feelings. And the better we know His Word, the more clearly we will know His will.

Unfortunately, a person may actually know the Scriptures and yet not really know them. That is, a person may intellectually know what the Bible says, and may even have memorised it from cover to cover, yet still be oblivious to its real meaning. If he has not "made it his own" through obedience to it, he won't even understand what the Bible is all about. I have met men with theological degrees who knew all about the history, geography and literary merits of the Bible, but who had no more idea of its inner message than, as we say, "the man in the moon".

Three steps

There are three steps we must take to profit from God's Word. Step one is to hear the truth. This means that you have to do more than just read these notes, you must read the Bible itself. Step two is to believe the truth. This means accepting its message as from God. Step three is to practise truth. This means doing whatever God asks you to do, whether you feel like it or not. The Amplified Bible's rendering of John chapter 8, verse 31 reads: "If you abide in my word – hold fast to my teachings and live in accordance with them. . ."

The result of these three steps is understanding the truth, and when we understand His truth we are better able to understand His will for our lives. Note, however, that full understanding comes only after obedience. Our lives must be guided by God's Word, checked at every point by His Word, fed by His Word and characterised by obedience to His Word. Then, and only then, are we in a position to specifically seek God's will and guidance regarding any particular issue.

Words of caution

Before going on to consider how to use God's Word correctly in guidance, we pause to consider how it is often incorrectly used. Many Christians use their Bible like a lucky dip. They keep it on the shelf until an emergency occurs, and then bring it down, open up a page at random and take the first thing they read to be God's direction. This is often referred to as "the finger-pointing method". You must have heard the classic story of the man who, caught up in a serious crisis, and seeking guidance by this means, let his Bible flip open and put his finger on the first verse he came to. It read: "And Judas went and hanged himself." That can't be right, he thought, so he tried again. This time he read: "Go, and do thou likewise." Still not having learned his lesson, he tried one more time. This is what he read: "What thou doest, do quickly."

This practice of opening the Bible at random and receiving the first word one reads as a personal divine message has brought about much harm. I am not saying that God has never used His Word in this way to guide His children, for John Wesley occasionally used this method. With him, however, it was never a substitute for close study of the Scriptures, and he did it only when his mind was overwrought. It is said that on the morning of 24th May 1738, he opened up his New Testament at random and read these words: "Thou art not far from the kingdom of God." At a quarter to nine the same evening, the great experience came. Although God may sometimes use His Word in this way to speak to His children, it must never become a substitute for the close and careful study of the Scriptures.

Another caution to bear in mind is the tendency some Christians have to make the Bible mean what they want it to mean. This is why we can never understand the Bible correctly until we are willing to submit our own will and desires to the will of God. If we don't, then we can very easily see in a text only that which supports our self-centred ends. The cults do this all the time. Guidance cannot come until the self is surrendered, and the life is shifted from self-will to God's will. Don't be tempted to think the end justifies the means, and misuse passages to gain your own ends, rather than God's ends.

Be careful, too, of the danger of always wanting a Bible text to support every decision you make. Some Christians say: "Search the Bible for a word which exactly fits your situation, and never do anything until you have one." It is good to have a firm scriptural basis, but the idea of always being able to find a specific verse which is exactly applicable to any given situation leads to a distortion of Scripture. Paul didn't have a verse to support every move he made: "I planned to visit you on my way to Macedonia and to come back to you from Macedonia. . ." (v.16: NIV). I heard of one Christian who, prior to voting day, searched for a Bible verse to help him decide for whom he should vote. He read in the Old Testament that David was chosen to be a king over his taller brothers, and concluded that this meant he should vote for the shortest candidate!

The path to maximum guidance

We are seeing that the Bible is God's chief way of guiding and directing His people toward His will for their lives. Obviously, this means that, as far as the Book is concerned, God can guide most those who read it most. How, then, shall we read the Bible to get the maximum guidance from its pages?

First

First, we must study it with *prayer*. As we take it in hand, let us remember that this Book was written by men who were specially guided by the Holy Spirit, and it will only be understood, in all its richness, by those who have the same divine help.

Second

Second, we must read it every day, *unhurriedly*. Of course, as I have said so many times before, we must not get into bondage about this and think that if we miss one day's Bible reading because of some emergency, God is going to withdraw His presence from us. Remember God is your *Father*. Would any human father act like that? But do make it a goal to read it every day in a relaxed and unhurried way. You are most receptive when you are relaxed. Nothing can be inscribed on a tense and anxious mind. Little value can be derived from a chapter hurriedly scanned, and the mind diverted at once to something else.

Third

Third, ask yourself two vital questions in relation to every verse or passage you read: what did it mean when it was first written? What does it mean for me now? Sometimes the two answers will coincide. Sometimes the answer to the first question will elude you, and yet the passage can still have personal worth. Nobody who seeks divine guidance can neglect the richest and surest way to it, the daily reading of the Scriptures.

Fourth

Fourth, learn how to retain key passages of Scripture by committing them to memory. I was in a church some time ago when a young man reading the lesson spoke these words: "You shall hate all men for my name's sake." One or two lifted their eyebrows, but most of the congregation showed no surprise. Most of them, I concluded, didn't know the correct reading, which is "You shall be hated of all men for my name's sake" (Luke 21:17). I am more and more concerned that the generation in which we are now living seems not to be trained in memorising Scripture, and it is mentally and morally the poorer as a result. May I make a suggestion? Over the next seven days, commit a verse to memory each day, and see if your spiritual life is not the richer. Don't just take any text of the Bible, but select one that has a special and personal meaning for you.

Fifth

Fifth, if some verse or passage speaks to your condition, then roll it round and round in your mind. This is called "meditation", a principle which, I am afraid, is only really understood by about one in a thousand Christians. Turning Scripture over and over in your mind enables the Word of God to produce an atmosphere within your soul. The atmosphere becomes an attitude, and the attitude soon becomes an act. When Jesus was hard-pressed by the temptations in the wilderness, He answered in the words of Scripture. The words He used had become part of Him, and, in the crisis, they naturally passed from the stage of assimilation and atmosphere to that of attitude and act.

Sixth

Sixth, let the Bible lead you to Christ's feet. Reading the Bible is not merely an intellectual exercise, it is a tryst with the Trinity. I heard a minister tell how he was sitting in a train one day reading the Bible, when a bright-faced, oldish lady opposite him blurted out, "Oh, you must love the Author, for you are reading His Word. I, too, love the Author." "At once," he said, "we were friends around *the* Friend." In reading the Word, remember that what you have read is leading you to His feet. Upon Him all the Old Testament truths converge: from Him all the New Testament truths emerge. He is the centre of gravity of the Bible; look for Him when you are reading its pages."

Seventh

Seventh, as you read the Word, keep realigning your life with Christ's life. In Korea, a girl did not come back for more instruction in Scripture and when asked why, she replied, "I haven't learned to practise fully what I have been taught." She felt she had to keep abreast of the teaching and she was right. A Negro preacher prayed, "Lord, prop us up on our leaning side." Re-align your life every day with His.

Eighth

Eighth, if something gets hold of you when you are reading Scripture, pass it on to someone else the same day. I stressed this point several years ago in my writings, and a woman wrote to me and said: "That was the best piece of advice I have ever received in my whole life. I learned that I never really fully understood a truth until I shared it. In the sharing, the meaning and impact become more real." Repetition helps retention, and what is more, it helps brighten the path of another.

CHAPTER 5

IN
HIS
IMAGE

"So God created man in his own image, in the image of God he created him. . ." (Genesis 1:27, NIV)

The Bible is the cornerstone of guidance, and the more we know and understand God's Word, the more effectively we can be guided. Before we go on to see how Biblical principles can operate in our lives to help us correctly decide things that are not covered by Scripture, we need to consider the issue of individual freedom. We ask ourselves, therefore: how much freedom does God give us in making decisions over things that are outside the scope of Scripture? As the way we perceive our individual freedom has a direct bearing on our views concerning guidance, we must try to think this through.

Free to choose

When God created man He made him in His own image. That image accounts for man's great value to God and distinguishes him from all other creatures. Man alone was invested with the determinative features of personality: intellect, emotion and will. And only man was given a position of responsibility, requiring the exercise of those attributes. If we were to make our decisions based on instinct, as do the animals, we would be no different from them.

Or if we required direct input from our Creator for every decision we are called upon to make, then we would be no more than manipulated robots. One writer puts it like this: "By God's design, only the image-bearer (man) approaches decisions in the same manner as the Creator." What a risk God took in making us like Himself. Inevitably. But He took it. God, being the loving Being He is, could not do otherwise. Dr John White, in his book *The Cost of Commitment*, put it most effectively when he said: "Within boundaries prescribed by God's own character, man analyses, evaluates, judges and *freely determines* (italics mine) his choices."

The principle of freedom of choice was clearly part of the Creator's design from the very beginning:

"This is the account of the heavens and the earth when they were created.

When the Lord God made the earth and the heavens, no shrub of the field had yet appeared on the earth and no plant of the field had yet sprung up; the Lord God had not sent rain on the earth and there was no man to work the ground, but streams came up from the earth and watered the whole surface of the ground. And the Lord God formed man from the dust of the ground and breathed into his nostrils the breath of life, and man became a living being.

The Lord God took the man and put him in the Garden of Eden to work it and take care of it. And the Lord God commanded the man, "You are free to eat from any tree in the garden; but you must not eat from the tree of the knowledge of good and

evil, for when you eat of it you will surely die.'"
(Genesis 2:4–7, 15–17, NIV).

It is stated in the very first commandment that was given to man: "You are *free* to eat from *any* tree in the garden." Adam and Eve were free to partake of any of the fruit that grew in the Garden of Eden, and were limited by only one restriction: "But you must not eat from the tree of the knowledge of good and evil." In this very first commandment, man's freedom to choose was categorically asserted, and provided in advance a rebuttal of Satan's allegation that God is a tyrant:

"Now the serpent was more crafty than any of the wild animals the Lord God had made. He said to the woman, 'Did God really say, You must not eat from any tree in the garden?'
The woman said to the serpent, 'We may eat fruit from the trees in the garden, but God did say, You must not eat fruit from the tree that is in the middle of the garden, and you must not touch it, or you will die.'
'You will not surely die,' the serpent said to the woman. 'For God knows that when you eat of it your eyes will be opened, and you will be like God, knowing good and evil.'" (Genesis 3:1–5, NIV).

Free within limits

The freedom that man has, however, is not an unlimited freedom. In fact, there is no such thing as "unlimited freedom". The freest birds do not have it, they can fly only to certain heights; the oceans do not have it, they are bounded by the coastline; and neither does man have it. We are free only within certain limits. You are perfectly free, for example, to jump off the roof of a ten-storey building, but after you have jumped you are no longer free. You will be caught in the grip of gravity and brought swiftly to the ground. So mark this and mark it well: you are free, but free only within limits. Someone put it like this: "My freedom to swing my arm ends at the tip of your nose." We are free to swing our arms, but not to misuse our freedom by hurting others. If there were no limits to freedom, then freedom would soon become lawlessness.

In the car park at one of CWR's former headquarters, there was a section which was reserved for vehicles belonging to the staff. It was clearly marked "CWR Parking", and was part of the terms of the agreement by which CWR rented office space in the building. Sometimes other people parked in these reserved spaces, and one such person, when gently and courteously told that he was infringing the rights of others, replied: "But it's a free country." His view of freedom was that he could do what he liked. If that idea was carried to its logical conclusion, then society would end up in anarchy.

People are free, of course, to go beyond the limits set by rules or law, but they are not free to choose the consequences of their actions. Once they have misused their freedom in transgressing the prescribed boundaries, then they have to face the consequences of their actions, and in that realm they have no further individual choice. Freedom without law becomes lawlessness.

Man was given the freedom to make free judgments, but he was also given the dignity of bearing full responsibility for the consequences of his choices. Adam was free to sin, but he was not free to choose the consequences of his sin. God said: ". . . for when you eat of it you will surely die" (Genesis 2:17, NIV). It happened precisely as God said. Adam died spiritually the moment he sinned, and he began also to die physically.

Freedom continued

Does that mean that, after Adam sinned, the principle of freedom was revoked? No. It did require, however, a more extensive revelation of God's moral will and character. The human heart is now tainted with sin, and has a bias that moves it away from God, so the area of freedom becomes more restricted as the limits of God's moral will are set out.

The principle of freedom, although more constricted and narrowed down as a result of Adam's sin, remained in force even under the Law. Take the example of a freewill offering. A freewill offering is a Scriptural exercise: ". . . If any of you . . . presents a gift for a burnt offering to the Lord, either to fulfil a vow or as a freewill offering" (Leviticus 22:18, NIV). Man could ask: "Is it God's will for me to give a freewill offering today?" If God answered, then the offering would no longer be one of freewill. God wanted to give His people some way in which they could express their voluntary devotion to Him. So He provided the option of the freewill offering and explained which sacrifices would be acceptable for this purpose.

The line of reasoning we are following is one that demands some close thinking, but it is important to grasp it if we are to properly understand the subject of divine guidance. We are saying that God has given us a certain degree of freedom in life, and we are attempting to prove that point from Scripture. We saw that Adam had it: "You are *free* to eat from *any* tree in the garden"; and that God maintained that principle in human life even after Adam sinned, which may be deduced from the institution of the "freewill offering".

There are many other Old Testament Scriptures that could be examined to prove this point. Look up Leviticus chapter 11, Deuteronomy chapter 18 vv 6–7 and chapter 23 vv 15–16 and vv 21–23. However, we should also look at a New Testament passage to see how this principle is further sustained. In Matthew chapter 20 vv 1–16, Jesus teaches:

"The kingdom of heaven is like a landowner who went out early in the morning to hire men to work in his vineyard. He agreed to pay them a denarius for the day and sent them into his vineyard. About the third hour he went out and saw others standing in the market-place doing nothing. He told them, 'You also go and work in my vineyard, and I will pay you whatever is right.' So they went. He went out again about the sixth hour and the ninth hour and did the same thing. About the eleventh hour he went out and found still others standing around. He asked them, 'Why have you been standing here all day long doing nothing?' 'Because no one has hired us,' they answered. He said to them, 'You also go and work in my vineyard.' When evening came, the owner of the vineyard said to his fore- man, 'Call the workers and pay them their wages, beginning with the last ones hired and going on to the first.' The workers who were hired about the eleventh hour came and each received a denarius. So when those came who were hired first, they expected to receive more. But each one of them also received a denarius. When they received it, they began to grumble against the landowner. 'These men who were hired last worked only one hour,' they said, 'and you have made them equal to us who have borne the burden of the work and the heat of the day.' But he answered one of them, 'Friend, I am not being unfair to you. Didn't you agree to work for a denarius? Take your pay and go. I want to give the man who was hired last the same as I gave you. Don't I have the right to do what I want with my own money? Or are you envious because I am generous?' So the last will be first, and the first will be last" (vv. 1–16, NIV).

The landowner was free to do what he did, provid- ing he stayed within the boundaries of fairness and justice. Some may think what he did was not just, but Jesus obviously thought it was. He was bound by the rules of fairness, but free to pay more than a fair wage if he chose to do so. The parable illustrates, of course, how God deals generously with all who enter His Kingdom. And there is no law against generosity!

Come to dinner!

We are coming to the conclusion that the principle of freedom was not only established in the Garden of Eden, but continued, with greater restrictions because of sin, after the Fall. Examples are abundant. Perhaps the clearest evidence of this can be seen in relation to the matter of food. The subject of food, a matter of importance in the Garden of Eden, as well as in ancient Israel, reappears as a topic for discussion in the early Church.

"Everything is permissible – but not everything is beneficial. Everything is permissible – but not everything is constructive. Nobody should seek his own good, but the good of others. Eat anything sold in the meat market without raising questions of conscience, for, 'The earth is the Lord's, and everything in it.' If some unbeliever invites you to a meal and you want to go, eat whatever is put before you without raising questions of conscience. But if anyone says to you, 'This has been offered in sacrifice,' then do not eat it, both for the sake of the man who told you and for conscience' sake – the other man's conscience, I mean, not yours. For why should my freedom be judged by another's conscience? If I take part in the meal with thankfulness, why am I denounced because of something I thank God for? So whether you eat or drink or whatever you do, do it all for the glory of God. Do not cause anyone to stumble, whether Jews, Greeks or the church of God – even as I try to please everybody in every way. For I am not seeking my own good but the good of many, so that they may be saved" (1 Corinthians 10:23–33, NIV).

A question had arisen in the Corinthian church in relation to eating meat that was sold in the market place after it had been offered to idols. Was this an issue about which there was a definite divine command? No. Then how was a believer to act if he accepted an invitation to a meal from an unbeliever, and then suspected that he was being offered "idol" meat?

Notice Paul does not say, "If an unbeliever asks you to come to dinner, pray about it and determine whether it is God's will for you to go," but rather, "If some unbeliever invites you to a meal and *you want to go*, eat whatever is put before you without raising questions of conscience." A believer is free to accept or decline an invitation according to his natural desire. Once he makes the decision to go, however, he is then under a Scriptural obligation not to probe the meal's pedigree or recent history for the sake of his conscience. Since there is no moral issue involved with the eating of the meat itself, the Christian is given the prerogative of choice. He is free to make up his mind whether or not to accept an invitation, but not free to refuse the meat on the grounds that it offends him. Although God surrounds us with clear guidelines and prescribed limits, within those limits we are accorded a good deal of personal freedom. As we said earlier, God wants to guide us, but not to override us.

In the days when horses were taken down into the coal mines, they were rarely driven from behind. The driver, or leader, would walk beside the horse and lead it wherever he wanted it to go. This close leading of the horse, however, took away its initiative and the horses tended to lose their spirit; they became helpless and over-dependent. To correct this, every now and again they had to bring the horses up to the surface and allow them to run free. In this way, they regained their spirit and recovered some of their initiative.

Independently dependent

God won't weaken us by imposing Himself upon every decision we have to make. He guides, but not in a way that cripples our initiative. Take another illustration: the father who takes his child's development seriously seeks to give him or her as wide a scope as possible for the exercise of judgment and decision-making. He is quick with words of counsel, which his love and experience qualify him to give, but as children grow and develop, they come to a time when they need less and less of their father's *active* counsel and support. The father who does everything for his child, dictating every least thing they should do throughout the day, weakens, not strengthens, that child. We, of course, as God's children, can never grow beyond His help, but He does want to develop us so that we learn to be independently dependent.

CHAPTER 6

GAINING WISDOM

". . . we have not stopped praying for you and asking God to fill you with the knowledge of his will through all spiritual wisdom and understanding." (Colossians 1:9, NIV)

Now that we have firmly established the fact that there is a good deal of freedom in life, we move on now to consider the question: how can we make sure that our free decisions are the right ones?

There are some who say that in an area which has no clear Scriptural principle governing it, you should go ahead, make the best decision you can, and whatever you decide will be acceptable to God. It is part of your freedom, they say, to make some choices on your own, and at such times you must not wallow in indecisiveness, but make up your own mind based on the options before you.

That seems like good advice as far as it goes, but it leaves out an important factor. While it is true that God allows us a good deal of freedom in life, we must seek to exercise this freedom with a sense of responsibility. No Christian should adopt the attitude, when he faces a situation which is not covered by a verse or passage in the Word of God, such as: whom shall I marry? what vocation should I choose? how many children should I have? and so on, that his spirituality can be suspended and that he can make his decision without recourse to any spiritual principle.

Wisdom is the key

There is one principle which takes precedence over all others when it comes to decision-making in areas that are not directly covered by Scripture, and that principle is contained in a word which appears in the Bible, in various forms, over five hundred times. What is that word? – *wisdom*. God wants us to develop spiritual wisdom so that when we are faced with decisions in the non-moral areas of our lives, we are able to make wise and prudent choices.

This raises the question: what is wisdom? J.B. Phillips gives an excellent perspective on it when he translates Colossians 1:9 in this way: "We are asking God that you may see things, as it were, *from His point of view* by being given spiritual insight and understanding." Wisdom can be defined quite accurately as "seeing things from God's point of view". Dr J.I. Packer, in his book *Knowing God*, gives the following definition: "Wisdom is the power to see, and the inclination to choose, the best and highest goal, together with the surest means of attaining it." Wisdom, quite simply, is the ability to figure out what is the best thing to do in any given situation.

How do we find it?

The next question we must face is this: how do we go about acquiring wisdom? I should point out at this stage that Scripture identifies two types of wisdom that we need to cultivate: spiritual wisdom and supernatural wisdom. Spiritual wisdom comes from assimilating the truths and principles of Scripture;

supernatural wisdom comes through the miraculous intervention of the Spirit in our lives. We shall look a little later at the subject of supernatural wisdom, but right now, let's begin our quest for spiritual wisdom by opening our hearts to God in this special prayer:

PRAYER

Gracious Father, I come to You with the utmost humility and ask You to make me a wise person. I need so desperately to be able to see life from Your point of view. Show me the steps that are necessary to attain spiritual wisdom, and help me to take each one – with no drawing back. Amen.

Proverbs chapter 8 verse 17 tells us that in relation to wisdom, those who seek shall find: "I love those who love me, and those who seek me find me." The key to acquiring wisdom is to know where to find it and how to look for it.

Soaked in the Scriptures

Firstly, *where* do we find it? The major source of spiritual wisdom lies in soaking oneself in the Scriptures. Let there be no mistake about this. Spiritual wisdom is not the result of good training or the learning of techniques; it comes from exposing oneself to the wisdom that flows through every page of the Scriptures. I have known believers, highly trained in the skills of decision-making, who made huge blunders in their Christian lives. They had plenty of knowledge, but lacked wisdom. One definition of wisdom says that it is "the ability to put knowledge to its best effect".

The process of gaining wisdom, as we shall see, contains a number of elements, the first of which is exposing our minds to God's eternal Word. We talked earlier about the importance of reading God's Word, and reading it daily, but now we must go one stage further and emphasise the importance of studying the Word of God. Study requires effort, but the effort, in turn, produces spiritual wisdom. Few Christians, it seems, are willing to put any effort into serious study of the Bible. They make do with devotional aids such as *Every Day with Jesus*, but have no form of systematic study by which they *search* the Scriptures. I sincerely hope that guides such as *Every Day with Jesus* will help you in your devotional life, but, quite honestly, I feel it fails if it does not prod you toward a more diligent study of the Word of God.

It is every Christian's responsibility to get to know as much about the Bible as they can. This includes reading: "Until I come, devote yourself to the public reading of Scripture..." (1 Timothy 4:13, NIV), careful consideration: "Reflect on what I am saying, for the Lord will give you insight into all this" (2 Timothy 2:7, NIV), searching and enquiry: "Concerning this salvation, the prophets, who spoke of the grace that was to come to you, searched intently and with the greatest care, trying to find out the time and circumstances to which the Spirit of Christ in them was pointing when he predicted the sufferings of Christ and the glories that would follow" (1 Peter 1:10–11, NIV).

It requires diligence in study: "Do your best to

present yourself to God as one approved, a workman who does not need to be ashamed and who correctly handles the word of truth" (2 Timothy 2:15, NIV), meditation: "But his delight is in the law of the Lord, and on his law he meditates day and night" (Psalm 1:2, NIV), memorisation: "I have hidden your word in my heart that I might not sin against you" (Psalm 119:11, NIV).

It means learning from gifted Bible teachers in both oral and written form: "Whatever you have learned or received or heard from me, or seen in me – put it into practice. And the God of peace will be with you" (Philippians 4:9, NIV); "And in the church God has appointed first of all apostles, second prophets, third teachers. . ." (1 Corinthians 12:28, NIV); "Anyone who receives instruction in the word must share all good things with his instructor" (Galatians 6:6, NIV).

Translate into action

Strange as it may sound, spiritual wisdom does not flow from a mere *study* of the Scriptures, it comes only as we *obey* it. "Now that you know these things," said Jesus, "you will be blessed *if you do them*" (John 13:17, NIV). In the early Church, there was a big discussion over whether a Gentile believer should become circumcised or remain uncircumcised. Many regarded it as a tremendously important issue. But listen to how the apostle Paul deals with this in one of his letters: "Circumcision is nothing and uncircumcision is nothing. *Keeping God's commands is what counts*" (1 Corinthians 7:19, NIV).

From the beginning of time, God has stressed the

importance of obedience as being the key to spiritual development and wisdom. Listen to what God told Joshua, a man of wisdom if there ever was one: "Do not let this Book of the Law depart from your mouth; meditate on it day and night, so that you may be careful to do everything written in it. Then you will be prosperous and successful" (Joshua 1:8, NIV). We should not just study Scripture, but obey it.

Wise up!

Every Christian ought to be committed to the goal of making wise decisions. You may feel greatly threatened by this statement, due, perhaps, to a poor education and lack of decision-making skills. Let me assure you that if you follow the Bible's prescription for obtaining wisdom, then no matter how limited your education or how poor your ability to make good decisions, you have God's promise that He will make you into a wise person. We have identified that the first step in obtaining wisdom is to read, study and meditate in the Scriptures. The more we do this, the more the wisdom of this wonderful Book will be absorbed into our spiritual bloodstream.

Develop the hunger

The second step to obtaining wisdom is to develop the attitude that wisdom is so valuable you will do everything humanly possible to obtain it. This means you will need to reflect on the value and importance of spiritual wisdom. Reflect on the fact that, as far as spiritual things are concerned, no man is wise in himself: "Do not be wise in your own eyes; fear the Lord and shun evil" (Proverbs 3:7, NIV) and, therefore, if he is to gain wisdom, it has to come from somewhere outside of himself. That "somewhere", of course, is God.

Our attitude must mirror the conviction that the source of wisdom is God alone. If we do not admit this, then we are self-deceived fools: "For although they knew God, they neither glorified him as God nor gave thanks to him, but their thinking became futile and their foolish hearts were darkened. Although they claimed to be wise, they became fools" (Romans 1:21–22, NIV). Wherever you look in Scripture, you will find that the attitude of the one who receives wisdom is that of reverence, humility, teachableness, diligence, uprightness and faith. The man or woman in whom wisdom is found is a person who bows humbly at the feet of the Creator.

Pray and look

The third step towards gaining wisdom is to *pray for it*. It is true that God's major way of imparting wisdom is through His Word, the Bible, but it is not His only way. He gives it also through the avenue of believing prayer. The fourth step in obtaining wisdom is to *look out at life*. The author of Proverbs, the textbook on obtaining wisdom, makes the point that God has built wisdom into nature, and that people would do well to reflect on the things which animals do by instinct.

"Four things on earth are small, yet they are extremely wise: Ants are creatures of little strength,

yet they store up their food in the summer; conies
are creatures of little power, yet they make their
home in the crags; locusts have no king, yet they
advance together in ranks; a lizard can be caught
with the hand, yet it is found in kings' palaces"
(Proverbs 30:24–28, NIV).

The importance of obtaining wisdom by observing
the habits of certain animals has been greatly over-
looked by the Christian Church.

"But ask the animals, and they will teach you, or
the birds of the air, and they will tell you; or speak
to the earth, and it will teach you, or let the fish of
the sea inform you" (Job 12:7–8, NIV).

The wisdom which God gave to Solomon included
a thorough understanding of the world of nature:
"He described plant life, from the cedar of Lebanon
to the hyssop that grows out of walls. He also taught
about animals and birds, reptiles and fish. Men of all
nations came to listen to Solomon's wisdom, sent by
all the kings of the world, who had heard of his
wisdom" (1 Kings 4:33–34, NIV). Adam's first task in
the Garden of Eden was to name each animal as God
brought them to him. He would never have been able
to give them precise names if he had not thoroughly
understood their ways. In Scripture, God assumes
that we know the ways of animals. If we do not know
something of the behaviour of bears, we will neither
appreciate nor understand the warning, "Better to
meet a bear robbed of her cubs than a fool in his folly"
(Proverbs 17:12, NIV).

Take wise advice

The fifth and final step in obtaining wisdom is to *discuss important issues with a wise spiritual counsellor*. The book of Proverbs stresses the importance and value of wise counsellors to the decision-maker: "For lack of guidance a nation falls, but many advisers make victory sure" (Proverbs 11:14, NIV). "The way of a fool seems right to him, but a wise man listens to advice" (Proverbs 12:15, NIV). "Pride only breeds quarrels, but wisdom is found in those who take advice" (Proverbs 13:10, NIV). "He who walks with the wise grows wise, but a companion of fools suffers harm" (Proverbs 13:20, NIV). In seeking to add to your wisdom, and especially before making an important decision, talk the situation over with a wise and caring Christian friend. The kind of person you should look for is one who has the reputation of possessing deep spiritual insight, and who has gone through a good many relevant experiences. Incidentally, if you want to be a counsellor, then be prepared to face all kinds of problems, because it is in the "University of Adversity" that God trains His counsellors. ". . . who comforts us in all our troubles, so that we can comfort those in any trouble with the comfort we ourselves have received from God" (2 Corinthians 1:4, NIV). He puts His counsellors into all kinds of difficult situations so that they can first experience His comfort and wisdom themselves, and then pass it on to others.

Let's now try to sum up what we have been saying before we move on to consider other aspects of our theme. We began by asking: how can we be sure that our free decisions are the right ones? The key, we discovered, lies in obtaining spiritual wisdom. God's chief way of imparting His wisdom to our minds is through His Word, the Bible. The more we study it, and obey it, the more the wisdom from this wonderful Book flows into our spiritual bloodstream. God mediates His wisdom to us in other ways as well, through the development of right attitudes, through prayer, through nature, and through the counsel of wise and mature Christians.

CHAPTER 7

MORE
THAN
CIRCUMSTANTIAL
EVIDENCE

"For it is God who works in you to will and to act according to his good purpose." (Philippians 2:13, NIV)

In the previous chapters, we have been stressing the fact that the Bible is God's chief method for guiding and directing our lives. In Scripture we have *all* we need to know in order to live an effective Christian life, and when called upon to make decisions that are not covered by a Biblical statement or passage, we apply to such decisions the wisdom we have derived from our exposure to God and His Word. The question we now ask ourselves is this: what other forms of guidance does God use to help us when we come to a crossroad and don't know which way to go?

Circumstances

One way is through *circumstances*. A Christian knows that God is sovereign over all things, and that He can work in and through circumstances to bring about His will. At times, therefore, God will bring about unexpected, unlikely circumstances together, with precise timing, to reveal His will.

Circumstances by themselves, however, should not be accepted as clear indications of God's will, for some circumstances can mislead us, rather than lead us. When God spoke to Jonah and told him to go to Nineveh and tell the people to repent, the prophet took a route that led in the opposite direction. Circumstances seemed right for his escape: "But Jonah ran away from the Lord and headed for Tarshish. He went down to Joppa, where he found a ship bound for that port. After paying the fare, he went aboard and sailed for Tarshish to flee from the Lord" (Jonah 1:3, NIV). He found a ship going to Tarshish and discovered he had just the right fare! Some believers I know, whose lives are guided only by circumstances, would have said: "God must have changed His mind. He doesn't want me to go after all. Look, things are coming together perfectly." Circumstances should be looked at carefully, subjected to much prayer and discussed, if possible, with a wise and experienced fellow believer.

An inner voice

Guidance also comes through the witness of the Holy Spirit speaking directly to our hearts. In the first scene of Bernard Shaw's *Saint Joan*, Captain Robert de Baudricourt pours scorn on Joan's belief that she has heard a heavenly voice by saying, "Such voices come from your imagination." Joan's reply was this: "Of course; that is how the messages of God come to us."

Is that how God speaks to us? Through the imagination? I think not. Thousands of believers who have made a practice of listening to God claim they can distinguish between their own imagination and the impression of God's will. This comes, they say, as the result of long practice. The more we develop the "listening" side of prayer, the more our spirits are sensitised to hearing God's voice.

Here, again, I must add a word of caution. Many years ago I thought God had spoken to me about a certain issue, and it had all the marks of a genuine word from above. I rested my whole weight on it, and it let me down. My faith was shaken, but not shattered. I recognised that the voice I had heard was the one I wanted to hear; it was my own subconscious giving me what it knew I deeply desired. An exception like this does not discredit the principle, however, and the adventurous soul will not turn back because of the possibility of human error. Nowadays I am more careful and, because of that, more accurate in recognising God's voice. God does guide through an inner voice, but such guidance is given only to those who have practised quiet and patient waiting on Him, and know how to disentangle the voices of the subconscious from the voice of God: "My sheep listen to my voice; I know them, and they follow me" (John 10:27, NIV).

Reasoning

Wouldn't it be wonderful if all we had to do to be guided was simply to sit down quietly in God's presence and listen for His voice? It *sometimes* happens that way, but experience shows that it is not a fixed pattern. Sometimes God guides us through our mental processes, through hard thinking and reasoning.

I heard of a minister who received a "call" to another church, and took the matter to the Lord in prayer. The impression he got was that he must think it through, issue by issue and point by point. He reasoned that he would have a bigger stipend, more influence and access to academic circles, and, after a while, became convinced that he should accept. He continued thinking, however, and realised that he had been altogether too personal in his conclusions. He had not weighed one thing against another. What about his present ministry? Had he accomplished the work God had given him to do? As he weighed one thing against the other, he concluded that he should stay where he was. Speaking of the experience afterwards he said, "The more I reasoned, the clearer the issues became until the reasons for staying overwhelmed the reasons for going. My decision is completely reasonable as I see it in the light of God."

Reason is one of the highest human endowments, and God will not allow it to atrophy for want of use. And when a Christian is called upon to find God's guidance through reason, how much easier this is if our mind-set has been developed through consistent exposure to the principles of God's Word by daily reading, study and prayer. "... be constantly renewed in the spirit of your *mind* – having a fresh mental and spiritual attitude" (Ephesians 4:23, Amplified Bible).

Others

Sometimes guidance comes through a small fellowship group whose members are committed to each other's spiritual growth. I am thankful that increasingly, in churches of all denominations, believers are coming to see the importance of functioning together in small groups.

Every human eye, we are told, has a "blind spot". It is situated in the retina, at the point where the optic nerve enters, and is insensitive to light or colour. Sometimes in court a driver pleads, in explaining why an accident happened, that he was unable to see a certain object because its image had fallen upon his blind spot. It is not uncommon for our spiritual eyes to have "blind spots", and one of the gains of functioning in a committed group is that the things we cannot see ourselves can be pointed out and put right.

In a recent group meeting where I was present, I saw this form of guidance beautifully at work. A minister shared that he felt God was speaking to him about a certain task, but he wanted to know definitely if the impression was from God or from himself. Gently the group talked with him, and it soon became evident that the uncertainty the minister felt was not because of his unsureness of God's call, but because of a fear of failure. Once this was faced, the defences in his personality which were blocking the Spirit's leading were quietly and resolutely dismantled. He confessed that, through the group, he had been brought to a place of understanding and guidance that he had never before thought possible. If God cannot guide us when we are alone, perhaps because of our insensitivity or defensiveness, then He sometimes resorts to guiding us through a group. One way or another, He will get His message across to us.

Personal desires

Another way in which God sometimes guides is along the line of our personal desires. The thing we long to do is often the thing God wants us to do.

Many Bible teachers avoid even mentioning this form of guidance because it is so obviously fraught with problems. However, let's see if we can face these problems and think our way through them together.

One problem we can fall into is what is known as the "filthy rags" complex. The Bible says that our righteousness is like "filthy rags" (Isaiah 64:6), and some people assume from this that every single desire we have is a selfish one. If such a person really wants to do something, he is checked by the thought that, because he wants to do it, it is a selfish desire and cannot be God's will. It doesn't always follow, however, that a desire, springing up in our heart, is a selfish one. It *could* be a definite prompting of the Spirit.

Another problem in relation to our desires is what is often called the "identical twins" theory, which is the exact opposite of the "filthy rags" complex. This is based on Psalm 37:4, which says: "Delight yourself in the Lord and he will give you the desires of your heart" (NIV). Some Christians take this verse to mean that if they are really dedicated to the Lord, then their desires will always be identical with His desires. This view is inviting because it is always easier to determine our desires than to discover the Lord's will. The proper approach is a balance between the two. You should not think of your desires as being "filthy rags" or "identical twins", but as something in between. They need to be looked at, carefully considered, and prayed over.

Sight

God guides also through bringing us up against some opportunity or need. Many years ago, on the streets of London, a little waif sidled up to a man and said: "Do you want to see where we live?" The man assented, and went with the little waif into some alleyways where some boys were sleeping in boxes, huddled together to keep one another warm. The man sat there most of the night, and before morning came, he knew he belonged to those boys. His name was Barnardo, and he went on to set up the internationally famous Dr Barnardo's Homes. God's guidance was the opening of the doctor's eyes to see an urgent need.

It's amazing how all around us there are needs which we look at with our eyes, yet do not see, that is, *really see*. There comes a moment, however, when it seems as if the scales fall away, and the need takes on a perspective of which you were previously unaware. I do not believe, as do some, that the need is the call. I have looked upon many areas of need in my time, and wished that I had the ability and the capacity to meet them all, yet, as I have prayed, I have been led to focus on those areas of need to which I am best able to contribute.

Dick Sheppard, a famous evangelist of this century, said, "Christianity does not consist in abstaining from doing things no gentleman would think of doing, but in doing things that are unlikely to occur to anyone who is not in touch with the Spirit of Christ." In bringing you face to face with a need or an opportunity, the Spirit will quicken your imagination, and create a concern in your heart from which you cannot escape. When that happens, it is almost certain that you are being guided.

The supernatural

One more avenue through which God gives guidance is the supernatural. In this area we come to such things as supernatural dreams and visions, the appearance of angels, miraculous interventions or manifestations of the gifts of the Spirit such as the word of wisdom, prophecy and so on.

Some Christians believe, of course, that supernatural guidance was given only to the early Church, and that, after the initiation period described in the book of Acts, supernatural events and happenings were no longer needed. The view I have always taken of this matter is as follows: although God's usual way of guiding His people is through His Word, and in areas not covered by Scripture, by the impartation of spiritual wisdom, He does, at times, use supernatural means of guidance.

I have witnessed in my own life occasions when God has guided me through such supernatural things as prophecy, dreams and the word of wisdom. However, honesty compels me to admit that it has not been a normal, everyday occurrence. The same cautions must be applied to supernatural happenings that we applied to other means of guidance, namely, that if a supernatural event does not line up with the revealed will of God in Scripture, then it must be ignored. That means, if an angel taps you on the shoulder and commands you to do something which is contrary to the Word of God, forget it. God uses many forms of guidance, but the one authority by which all guidance is to be evaluated is, as we have been at pains to point out, God's eternal and infallible Word.

CHAPTER 8

LISTENING, LEARNING AND OBEYING

"Therefore, I urge you, brothers, in view of God's mercy, to offer your bodies as living sacrifices. . ." (Romans 12:1, NIV)

We come now to the final part in seeking to discover the Biblical principles that help us understand guidance along with the will of God. Our task from here on is to pull together the principles we have been examining in order to develop a strategy for discovering God's guidance in those areas of our lives which are not directly covered by a clear statement of Scripture. Keep in mind, however, that step-by-step answers and checklists are nothing more than helps. They can make a definite contribution, but they will never eliminate our need to walk by faith, keeping our eyes on Christ.

The steps I am about to go through are ones that I use in my own life to determine divine guidance, but, before I do so, there are several preparatory questions I must ask you. Firstly, are you a Christian, one who knows God personally through faith in Christ? The steps I am going to give are "family" principles that can only be applied by members of God's family. If you are not a Christian, then surrender your life to Christ right now. Bow your head, ask God to forgive your sin and invite Christ into your life to be your Lord and Saviour.

Secondly, are you in good health, physically and emotionally? If not, then you may have difficulty applying these guidelines with the level of sensitivity that is needed. You may need the help of your minister or a Christian friend in determining divine guidance. Thirdly, are you willing to do God's will when once it is clear to you? Settle this issue right now, for only those who are willing to do His will can fully know it.

We have one more issue to face before we begin laying down some guidelines for determining divine guidance. Do you regularly spend time with God in prayer and in the reading of the Scriptures? If you don't, then you will lack one of the most essential elements for understanding divine guidance, spiritual sensitivity and wisdom.

Assuming that you are a Christian with fairly good health, that you are willing to do God's will, once it is shown you, and you regularly spend time with God in prayer and reading His Word, we are now ready to focus on the steps we need to take when seeking to know God's will in matters that are not clearly covered in Scripture.

Step one: *Begin by praying that God will help you discern and discover His will*

Since God has an individual purpose for each life, we must become skilled in the art of finding out what that purpose is. When you pray for guidance, therefore, cultivate these three attitudes: listen, learn, obey. Some of us listen but won't learn, and some of us learn but won't obey. A dedicated Christian is one who listens, learns and obeys. If he does not approach God in that attitude, there will soon be nothing to listen to, or to learn, or to obey.

"Prayer," said someone, "is an imperative part of seeking God's will. It does for you what a garage mechanic does when he cleans the windscreen of your car. It allows you to see the road and the signs without distortion or distraction." Prayer, also, is like a rush of cool air from a rolled-down window. It brings the drowsy "driver" back to full alertness.

Step two: *Open your heart in willing submission to the Holy Spirit and invite Him to be your Counsellor and Guide*

The two greatest means of guidance God has given us are the Bible and the Holy Spirit. We have already emphasised the relevance of Scripture in the matter of guidance, now we focus on the person of the Holy Spirit. The Bible is our objective authority, the Holy Spirit our subjective authority. Throughout the centuries, the Church has always endeavoured to keep these complementary authorities in balance – the Spirit and the Word, the Word and the Spirit – and not emphasise one to the exclusion of the other.

Some Christians place all their emphasis upon the Word. Thus they fall prey to an arid intellectualism and rationalism; they have little sense of the Spirit's presence in their lives. For others it is the subjective experience alone that counts. They rely so heavily upon the Holy Spirit that the Bible, apart from a few proof texts, becomes a neglected book. These believers have no operative objective authority in their lives. Both positions are wrong. If you tell me the Holy Spirit is leading you in a certain direction or to a certain decision, I have a right to insist that you check this out with the Scriptures. I am assuming you have absolute confidence in God's Word. Now open your heart to the Spirit so that He might flow into you and through you to give you the help and guidance that you need.

Step three: *See if you can find a Biblical principle that clearly relates to the issue which is before you*

The Bible contains both precepts and principles. A precept is a clear and specific statement that takes all guesswork out of a situation, for example, "Flee from sexual immorality..." (1 Corinthians 6:18, NIV). Sexual immorality is never the will of God, never! But the Bible also contains principles, general guidelines, that assist us through the "grey" areas.

Some principles to employ in decision-making are these: Is my motive to bring glory to God? "... whatever you do, do it all for the glory of God" (1 Corinthians 10:31, NIV). Will what I am planning to do make me more effective for Christ? "And whatever you do, whether in word or deed, do it all in the name of the Lord Jesus, giving thanks to God the Father through him" (Colossians 3:17, NIV). Will my decision cause another Christian to stumble? "It is better not to eat meat or to drink wine or to do anything else that will cause your brother to fall" (Romans 14:21, NIV). Will it involve me in any kind of evil? "Avoid every kind of evil" (1 Thessalonians 5:22, NIV). Will it hinder or help my growth toward spiritual maturity? "Therefore, since we are surrounded by such a great cloud of witnesses, let us throw off everything that hinders and the sin that so easily entangles, and let us run with perseverance the race marked out for us" (Hebrews 12:1, NIV). Will it compromise me and affect my Christian testimony?

"Have nothing to do with the fruitless deeds of darkness, but rather expose them" (Ephesians 5:11, NIV).

There are scores of such principles in the Bible, so get to know them. I would recommend that you make a list of every Biblical principle you come across in your Bible reading. Then, when you are next faced with a difficult decision, the Holy Spirit will use your knowledge of the Scriptures to lead you to an awareness of how His general principles apply to your particular question or difficulty. As a Christian yielded to the Spirit of God, your conscience and spirit will respond. If you don't have all the answers through this method, you will know one thing at least, whether or not the matter is in line with God's Word.

Step four: *Ask yourself: is the issue that I am facing in line with my own personal desires?*

Many Christian teachers, in laying down principles for discerning divine guidance, leave this one out because, so they say, it is "loaded with difficulties". I accept that, but I think it is possible to work through those difficulties and arrive at a valid principle for determining God's will for our individual lives. In terms of guidance, this has great implications. It means that I don't have to distrust all my own feelings and inclinations. Some Christians, particularly those with strong feelings of inferiority and psychological guilt (I say "psychological guilt" because real guilt immediately dissolves after genuine repentance and confession), assume that what *they* want must always be the wrong thing.

We have already mentioned the two extremes into which a Christian can fall in relation to this, the "filthy rags" complex and the "identical twins" syndrome, so, in making this point, I am assuming you are a balanced Christian, with a healthy self-image, and that you have been on the Christian path for some time. If you are daily walking with God then, in general, your feelings, inclinations and ideas may well be Spirit-inspired. I say "may well be" because those feelings must be checked alongside the other guidelines I am presenting. Our own inclinations, therefore, must not be dismissed, but put in their proper context because, if we are in touch with God, those feelings represent the union of ourselves with His Spirit.

Step five: *Realise that the more important the decision you have to make, the more time should be given to it*

One should be careful and balanced about this, of course, because if some decisions are postponed long enough, the matter is decided by your indecisiveness. The Biblical principle governing this is found in Ephesians chapter 5 vv 15-16, "Look carefully then how you walk, not as unwise men but as wise, making the most of the time" (RSV). Incidentally, as you can see, making good use of our time is an important element in walking in wisdom. Insignificant and unimportant issues ought to be decided quickly. Big and far-reaching ones should be looked at a little longer, and all the issues carefully weighed up. Give yourself a deadline for the task.

This is what I sometimes do when called upon to make a big decision: I take a sheet of paper, and draw a line down the centre of the page from top to bottom. At the top of the left-hand column, I write the word 'Pro', and at the top of the right-hand column the word 'Con'. I then prayerfully consider and write down in the left-hand column all the positive aspects of the decision I am about to make. Then I go through a similar exercise thinking of all the negative aspects of the issue, and listing them in the right-hand column. If the issue is of great importance, I might even consider a 24-hour fast, together with prayer and meditation in the Scriptures, which greatly increases the sensitivity of the human spirit. When the deadline approaches and the decision has to be made, I go ahead and make it on the basis of what I have considered is best.

Step six: *If you feel that God's guidance is not becoming clear to you, then consider talking the matter over with a wise and experienced fellow-Christian*

King Solomon wrote: "The purposes of a man's heart are deep waters, but a man of understanding draws them out" (Proverbs 20:5, NIV). In addition, he also wrote: "As iron sharpens iron, so one man sharpens another. As water reflects a face, so a man's heart reflects the man" (Proverbs 27:17 & 19, NIV). When Moses was in difficulty because he couldn't cope with his increasing responsibilities in governing the Israelites, he received some wise advice from Jethro, his father-in-law. Jethro said: "You and these people who come to you will only wear yourselves out. The work is too heavy for you; you cannot handle it alone" (Exodus 18:18, NIV).

Almost everywhere we look in Scripture, we find passages that highlight the fact that believers ought to help and admonish one another. Listen to this: "Let the word of Christ dwell in you richly as you teach and *admonish* one another with all wisdom..." (Colossians 3:16, NIV). Young Christians ought almost always to check their guidance with an older and more experienced believer. Older women in the Church are told to instruct and encourage the younger women (Titus 2:3-5). I know the references above relate to teaching and sharing the principles of God's Word, but I think they could also mean the talking over of personal problems and issues such as decision-making and guidance. But how often is this done? Sadly, it is a greatly neglected ministry in the Church. Make no mistake about it, God uses others to help us know His desires.

Step seven: *Look to see if God is saying anything in and through your circumstances*

Since circumstances provide the context in which many decisions have to be made, they are a key source of information to the Christian who is seeking guidance. They must be evaluated, however, not on their own, but in line with other aspects of God's leading. Christians who depend on circumstances alone to guide them can fall into difficulties. Amazing coincidences happen every day, to Christians and non-Christians alike, and we must learn to "read" our circumstances aright, for, as we saw with Jonah, they do not always convey God's direction for our lives. This is why I say again, circumstances should be laid alongside other aspects of guidance, the inner witness, the principles of Scripture, the guidance of others and so on.

Be careful about attempting to "set up" situations in order to find guidance. One woman I know, who wanted guidance on a certain matter, said to herself: "If tomorrow morning the milkman leaves two bottles of milk instead of the usual one, then I will take it as

God's will that I should become a missionary." This is taking guidance through circumstances too far! It is legitimate, I believe, along with other guidelines, to look for God's direction through circumstances, but circumstances, because they can so easily be misread, must be only a part of guidance and not the whole.

Step eight: *Keep in mind that when spiritual guidance does not seem to make your pathway clear, God is always able to resort to supernatural guidance*

I define "spiritual guidance" as the guidance that comes through prayer, meditation in the Scriptures, reasoning with God, and so on, and "supernatural guidance" as the things God does to guide us which are outside His ordinary and usual methods. I refer to such things as visions, dreams, and so on. I strongly suspect that God works in supernatural ways when He is having trouble getting through to us along the usual channels, although I can't be entirely certain about that.

An interesting example of supernatural guidance is the vision that Paul received, which is reported in Acts chapter 16 verse 9, "During the night Paul had a vision of a man of Macedonia . . . begging him, 'Come over to Macedonia and help us.'" This brought about a change in his plans. You would think that if anyone planned his future in a spiritual way, it would be Paul. But here he seems to be moving in a direction other than that which God had planned for him, and so the Holy Spirit intervenes supernaturally and spectacularly to direct him into a new sphere of activity. It was exceptional guidance, and obviously not the kind that was an everyday occurrence in the life of the great apostle. I can think of a number of times in my life, and so, I am sure, can you, when, in facing a situation that was unclear, God finally revealed His purpose to me in a supernatural way. We should never forget that we are serving a miraculous God.

Step nine: *Learn the secret of a sanctified and properly used imagination*

It's interesting, as C.S. Lewis once observed, that in relation to most spiritual issues, Christians seem to fall into one of two extremes, either of taking things too far, or not far enough. Some Christians use their imagination too much and magnify their fears and uncertainties out of all proportion. Others fail to use their imagination at all, and thus are bereft of an important aspect of guidance.

Whenever you are faced with a situation in which there are several possible options, and, after applying the other methods I have suggested, you are still not certain which way to go, then try what is often called "the way of peace". Get alone with God, and prayerfully commit your way to Him. Then, in your imagination, go down each of the roads which are open to you. Visualise yourself in the various situations, one at a time, and see if you can determine in which one you experience the most peace.

This method is based on the premise that when we prayerfully apply our imagination to several options that are open to us, providing we are living in accordance with God's revealed will in the Bible, we can fully expect Him to flood our hearts with peace when we travel along the right option in our imagination. "And let the peace (soul harmony which comes) from the Christ rule (act as umpire continually) in your hearts..." (Colossians 3:15, Amplified Bible). This method should not be used alone, as I am continually seeking to stress, but when used alongside the other methods I have suggested, it is a valid means of supplementary guidance.

Step ten: *God never makes the path ahead absolutely clear because He wants us to exercise faith*

This applies not only to the unrevealed will of God, but also to His revealed will as laid out in the Bible: ". . . without faith it is impossible to please God. . ." (Hebrews 11:6, NIV). Many of the challenges God gives us in His Word require an act of faith and obedience before we can actually experience them in our lives. When I first read Romans chapters 6 and 7, and came across the principle of "reckoning myself dead to sin", I thought it was the most ridiculous thing I had ever heard. I remember saying to myself: how can the benefits of Christ's death on Calvary come to me simply by "reckoning" on it? Yet, as I took that principle by faith and acted on it, in an amazing way the light came on in my heart.

Sometimes the same thing happens in relation to guidance in the unrevealed areas of my life. I come to a point where I believe all the road signs are pointing in a certain direction, but then a doubt or an uncertainty creeps in and I am afraid to move. At such times I remind myself of this last principle, and providing I have checked out the other means of guidance, I take a step of faith into the unknown and trust God. The knowledge of God's will, both His revealed and unrevealed will, always calls for an act of faith as in obedience we move out into what, in some measure, is uncharted territory. How gratifying it becomes, however, when we look back in retrospect and say: "Yes, truly, God led me. That decision was most definitely His will."

CHAPTER 9

CONCLUDING
ENCOURAGEMENT

"You will keep on guiding me all my life with your wisdom and counsel; and afterwards receive me into the glories of heaven!" (Psalm 73:24, The Living Bible).

I feel God wants me to make the final word a word of encouragement, perplexing as many of the problems are in relation to this subject, and partial though our explanations may have been. In all great effort there comes a testing time, and in so great an enterprise as living the guided life, it comes again and again.

The discipline of daily prayer times may chafe you, especially during those "dry" periods which come to everyone, but the discipline must be endured in the sure knowledge that guidance, in its highest form, comes most clearly to those who soak their thoughts in God's Word and enjoy constant communion with Him. But do not just think of the discipline, think of the rewards. Is it not wonderful to walk through life feeling the certain pressure of His guiding hand? Is it not wonderful to be assured of the fact that, whether in sunshine or shade, He leads me? Is it not wonderful also to experience the security of knowing that, even when we might have made a wrong decision because of our human frailty, God is able, given our consent and co-operation, to bring our lives back on to the right course?

Amazing Love! How can it be? Take heart, my friend, the future need not frighten you. As you give your whole attention to the things that make you most responsive to His guidance, striving above all else for a greater sensitivity to His will, seeking you will find, and finding you will follow Him to the end, and beyond the end, where

> *"The invisible appears in sight*
> *And God is seen by mortal eye."*

PRAYER

Father, You have shown me the way – now help me to walk in it. Teach me to live in harmony with the central purpose of my existence, so that I can say, as did Your Son: "I have finished the work that You gave me to do." Amen.

IN HIS IMAGE IN HIS WORLD

A Biblical guide to today's issues

Editor: **Eddie Tait**

In three sections: The World, The Family, The Faith, *In His Image In His World* tackles many of the issues which challenge Christians today. Well-known writers take a fresh look at Scripture on topics like creation/evolution, the environment, politics and power, ethnic peoples, missions, marriage and divorce, sexual relationships, Christianity in the workplace and growing in faith. Eighteen subjects in eighteen chapters, each one divided into seven-day sections with Scripture readings and informed comment — an ideal guide for Bible Study groups or individuals to confront the issues of the 90s.

● Daily readings from the Bible
● Discussion starters for group use

"Bite-sized chunks of thoughtful Biblical material on vital issues. I would recommend it highly for individuals and small groups."
Stephen Gaukroger

"If you are looking for daily Bible-reading notes which cover politics, old age, the green issue and prosperity doctrine, along with 14 other topics, look no further . . . this book I liked!"
21st Century Christian

REVIVAL
Times of Refreshing
Selwyn Hughes

Without doubt one of the greatest themes of Scripture is "heaven-sent" revival.

"Heaven-sent" because real revival is not something that springs up or out of the normal activities of the Christian Church but something that comes down from above.

In *Revival — Times of Refreshing* Selwyn Hughes explores what revival is — and isn't. He looks at past revivals to examine how we, and the Church as a whole, are prepared by God for revival so that we may know how to respond.

Has God got something bigger in His heart for us than we are at present seeing? Yes, says Selwyn Hughes, God is able to do greater and yet more wondrous things. He has reserves of power which we, the Church of this generation, have not fully experienced. Our task is to lay hold on His highest willingness.